A Companion Guide to
Leadership for Safe Schools

Raymond Calabrese

With
Susan Allain, Jeanne Binovi,
Theresa Guadiano, William Ruff,
and Blane Trautwein

The Scarecrow Press, Inc.
A Scarecrow Education Book
Lanham, Maryland, and London
2002

SCARECROW PRESS, INC.

A Scarecrow Education Book

Published in the United States of America
by Scarecrow Press, Inc.
4720 Boston Way, Lanham, Maryland 20706
www.scarecroweducation.com

4 Pleydell Gardens, Folkestone
Kent CT20 2DN, England

British Library Cataloguing in Publication Information Available

Library of Congress Cataloging-in-Publication Data

Calabrese, Raymond L., 1942–
    A companion guide to Leadership for safe schools / Raymond L. Calabrese with Susan
Allain ... [et al.].
        p. cm.
    "A Scarecrow Education book."
    ISBN 0-8108-4205-X (pbk. : alk. paper)
    1. School violence—United States—Prevention. 2. Community and school—United
States. 3. Educational leadership—United States. 4. Meetings—Planning. I. Calabrese,
Raymond L., 1942– Leadership for safe schools. II. Title.

LB301.3 .C316 2002
371.7'82'0973—dc21   2001049548

♾™ The paper used in this publication meets the minimum requirements of American National Standard for Information Sciences—Permanence of Paper for Printed Library Materials, ANSI/NISO Z39.48-1992. Manufactured in the United States of America.

Contents

Preface

Susan Allain, Jeanne Binovi, Theresa Guadiano, William Ruff, and Blane Trautwein, the co-authors of this work, are doctoral students at The University of Texas at San Antonio. When I was a professor there, they were my students. They studied and applied my book *Leadership for Safe Schools: A Community-Based Approach*. Each student is currently an educational practitioner: school administrator, teacher, and university graduate assistant with public school experience. They came up with the excellent idea to develop a companion guide to the text. We formed a team to develop this workbook to facilitate the process of constructing a unique safe school plan for school administrators and staff development experts.

A Companion Guide to Leadership for Safe Schools aims the administrator and workshop facilitator in the right direction to broadly involve other people in developing and implementing a campus-level safe school plan. The school leader uses this guide in conjunction with the accompanying text, *Leadership for Safe Schools: A Community-Based Approach*. The text provides the background and foundation for the activities in this workbook.

Each workbook section is in a meeting format. Each meeting has a suggested time-frame. Within the meetings are group directed activities that are succinct and concise; these activities and the schedule keep the team on track. A reflective journal is provided after each meeting. Use of the journal will guide the school administrator and workshop facilitator toward constant quality improvement. This practice is also recommended for each member of the team. Following the progression of the workbook, one meeting and activity at a time yields a ready to implement safe school plan. Some schools may already have completed parts of this process. Administrators in these schools should move directly to the sections pertinent to their context.

Getting Ready

See *Leadership for Safe Schools* (*LSS*) pp. 14-16

1. **Assemble your team.**

2. **Choose constructive members who will contribute.**

   Some Important Characteristics to Consider

   - **Work ethic**
   - **Integrity**
   - **Commitment**
   - **Trustworthiness**
   - **Communication skills**

3. Create a list of potential members and analyze each member's strengths and weaknesses.

- **Include faculty, staff, and community.**

Name	Position	Strengths and Weaknesses	Respect of the Community	Positive Force
			YES NO	YES NO
			YES NO	YES NO
			YES NO	YES NO
			YES NO	YES NO
			YES NO	YES NO
			YES NO	YES NO
			YES NO	YES NO
			YES NO	YES NO
			YES NO	YES NO
			YES NO	YES NO

4. Publicly Announce the Members of the Team and the Team's Mission

Team Member	Affiliation
Ms. Merle Ferguson	PTA President

First Meeting: Claiming Your Identity

Approximate Meeting Length: One Hour

See *LSS*, pp. 7-9

Meeting Goals

Goal 1: Identify community characteristics.

- **Cultural**
- **Political**
- **Economic**

Goal 2: Provide teachers and administrators an opportunity to self-assess their responsibilities and duties in a safe school environment.

The Pathway to Achieving the Goals

Activity One (30 minutes)

Identify the school community's cultural, political, and economic values.

Create three subcommittees:

- **Cultural**
- **Political**
- **Economic**

Each subcommittee meets for 30 minutes to complete its task.

Subcommittee Tasks

Cultural Subcommittee

Task: Identify school and community cultures.

Culture can be an ethnic presence, socioeconomic group, or religious affiliation to which the majority of a community adheres.

1. Identify dominant school and community cultures.

School Cultural Context	Community Cultural Context
1.	1.
2.	2.
3.	3.
4.	4.

2. Identify potential leaders from the dominant school and community cultures who exert inordinate influence.

School Cultural Context	Community Cultural Context
1.	1.
2.	2.
3.	3.
4.	4.

3. Identify subcultures in your community or school.

Existing School Subcultures

Existing Community Subcultures

4. Identify potential leaders from the respective subcultures who will be critical to the subdominant culture's acceptance of the safe school plan developed by the committee.

Potential Leaders in School Subcultures

Potential Leaders in Community Subcultures

Political Subcommittee

Task: Identify political groups.

The purpose is to identify political forces that may contribute to the team. These may be (but are not limited to) teachers' unions, city leaders, and school board members.

1. **Identify a major political group and define the group's agenda and aspirations.**

_____
_____
_____
_____

2. **Identify another political group and define the group's agenda and aspirations.**

_____
_____
_____
_____

3. **Identify a final political group and define the group's agenda and aspirations.**

_____
_____
_____
_____

Economic Subcommittee

Task: Identify school community economic resources.

Identify groups that have strong influence over the underlying resources available in the community and the overall status of the community.

1. **Identify the average family income for your community.**

   Median High Income: _____

   Median Low Income: _____

2. Identify the following percentages of students enrolled in the school.

Low socioeconomic status students _____ %

Special education students _____ %

Gifted and talented students _____ %

Minority students _____ %

What Did We Learn?

1.

2.

3.

4.

5.

6.

7.

Activity Two ( Ten Minutes)

LEADER: Brainstorm characteristics of your safe school. Record the suggestions on a chart tablet and the final suggestions in this log.

Safe School Characteristics

_____

_____

_____

_____

_____

_____

_____

_____

_____

_____

_____

_____

_____

_____

_____

_____

_____

_____

_____

_____

_____

_____

_____

_____

_____

_____

_____

_____

Activity Three ( **20 Minutes)**

See *LSS*, pp. 17-19

Divide your team into three groups.

- **Group 1 identifies the important teacher characteristics for creating a safe school.**

- **Group 2 identifies the role of the administrator in the safe school.**

- **Group 3 identifies the joint roles of the teacher and administrator.**

This exercise enables the team to conduct a need assessment for the campus.

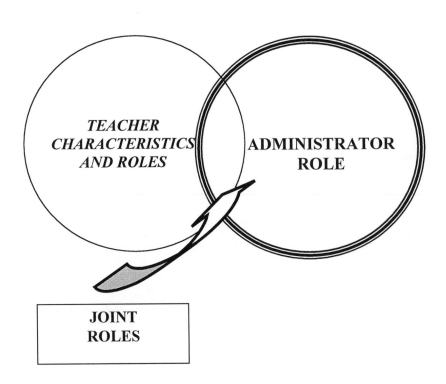

Checklist of Teacher Characteristics to Create/Sustain a Safe School Environment

Teachers	Exists	Does Not Exist
Form instructional groups that fit students' academic and affective needs		
Make efficient use of learning time		
Establish smooth, efficient classroom routines		
Set clear standards for classroom behavior and apply them fairly and consistently		
Carefully orient students to lessons		
Provide clear and focused instructions		
Routinely provide feedback to students and reinforcement regarding their learning process		
Review and teach to help all students master learning material		
Use validated strategies to build basic and higher level skills		
Use effective questioning techniques to build basic and higher level skills		
Integrate workplace readiness skills into content area instruction		
Hold high expectations for student learning		
Provide incentives, recognition, and rewards to promote excellence		
Give high-needs students the extra time and instruction they need to succeed		
Support the social academic resiliency of high-needs students		
Promote respect and empathy among students of different socioeconomic and cultural backgrounds		
Monitor student progress closely		
Make use of alternative assessments as well as traditional tests		
Interact with students in positive and caring ways		

Checklist for Administrator and Teacher Characteristics to Create/Sustain a Safe School Environment

Administrators and Teachers	Exists	Does Not Exist
Base curriculum planning on clear goals and objectives		
Integrate the curriculum as appropriate		
Provide computer technology for instructional support and workplace simulation		
Include workplace preparation among school goals		
Organize students to promote instruction		
Assure that school time is used for learning		
Establish and enforce clear, consistent discipline policies		
Provide a pleasant physical environment for teaching and learning		
Communicate high expectations for teacher performance		
Communicate high expectations to students and recognize excellent performance on a school-wide basis		
Provide programs and support to help high-needs students achieve school success		
Work to achieve equity in learning opportunities and outcomes		
Provide multicultural education activities as an integral part of school life		
Provide challenging academic content and English language skills for language minority students		
Identify dropout prone students and implement activities to keep them in school		
Use validated practices for tobacco, alcohol, and drug prevention		
Involve parents and community members in supporting the instructional program		
Involve parents and community members in school governance		

Checklist for Administrator Characteristics to Create/Sustain a Safe School Environment

Administrators	Exists	Does Not Exist
Undertake school restructuring efforts as needed to attain goals agreed upon for the students		
Display strong leadership in the instructional program		
Continually strive to improve instructional effectiveness		
Engage staff in professional development and collegial learning activities		
Communicate high expectations to students and recognize excellent performance on a school-wide basis		
Monitor student learning progress		
Develop and use alternative assessments		
Collaborate with community agencies to support families with urgent health and/or social service needs		

Did the team:

- **Identify each culture in the school community?**

- **Identify political groups in the school community?**

- **Identify school community economic resources?**

- **Identify the presence of characteristics in administrators and teachers?**

- **Provide teachers and administrators an opportunity to self-assess their responsibilities and duties in a safe school environment?**

Reflective Journal

Use this space to reflect on the first meeting. You may share these reflections during the first part of the next meeting.

_____
_____
_____
_____
_____
_____
_____
_____
_____
_____
_____
_____
_____
_____
_____
_____
_____
_____
_____
_____
_____
_____
_____
_____
_____
_____
_____
_____
_____
_____

Second Meeting: Identifying Values

Approximate Meeting Length: One Hour

See *LSS*, pp. 25-27

Meeting Goals

Goal 1: Identify personal and collective values.

Goal 2: Identify shared values.

Goal 3: Create team commitment and organizational boundaries.

Activity One (15 Minutes)

LEADER: In this activity, each member identifies his or her own personal values.

A value is an axiom, criterion, or attribute considered worthwhile or desirable by an individual or a team. Values serve as the standard for judging or directing our lives.

1. Give each team member ten rocks or other objects. Ask the members to assign a value to each object and write it down. (5 minutes)

2. Ask each member look at his or her list again, and then delete three values. (5 minutes)

3. Ask each member to examine his or her list again. Does this list reflect the most important personal values? (5 minutes)

Activity Two (20 minutes)

LEADER: Record and share the values of each team member.

1. **List the values identified by each team member.**

2. **Ask each person to explain why his or her identified value is important.**

3. **Look for similarities among values.**

4. **Compile shared values into one list.**

Shared Team Values

A. _____

B. _____

C. _____

D. _____

E. _____

Activity Three (15 Minutes)

See *LSS*, pp. 35-37

LEADER: Identify significant school community members and their roles and responsibilities in developing and/or implementing a safe school plan.

School Community Member	Identified Role and Responsibility in the Safe School
Principal	
Assistant Principal	
Teacher	
Teacher's Assistant	
Coach	
Counselor	
Nurse	
Secretary	
Custodian	
Student	
Parent	

Ask each member to think about his/her commitment to the process for the next meeting. List each member's commitment on an integrity check board during the next meeting. This is part of a Commitment Day activity. For further discussion, see chapter 2 in **LSS**.

Did the team:

- Identify their personal and collective values?

- Identify shared values?

- Identify the roles and responsibilities of school community members?

- Create team commitment and organizational boundaries?

Reflective Journal

Use this space to reflect on the second meeting. You may share these reflections during the first part of the next meeting.

_____
_____
_____
_____
_____
_____
_____
_____
_____
_____
_____
_____
_____
_____
_____
_____
_____
_____
_____
_____
_____
_____
_____
_____
_____
_____
_____
_____

Third Meeting: Committing to the Plan

Approximate Meeting Length: One Hour

See *LSS*, pp. 37-41

Meeting Goals

Goal 1: Share individual commitments to the safe school team.

Goal 2: Develop an integrity checklist for the team.

Goal 3: Generate a metaphor to create a shared vision.

Activity One (30 Minutes)

1. **The leader begins by sharing his/her commitment and listing it on a chart.**

(**Suggested statement: "I am committed to working with this team, students, teachers, and parents in a democratic process to develop an effective safe school plan. Even in times of disagreement, I am committed to working to find common ground. I will support each member of this team, and I will stay with the process. I will support the plan we develop, implement, and see it to its successful conclusion."**)

2. **Each team member shares his/her commitment to the process.**

3. Discuss the integrity check board and post it in a visible area in the meeting room. (For further explanation of the integrity board, see chapter 2 of *LSS*).

Integrity Check

Activity Two (30 Minutes)

See *LSS*, pp. 47-60

Generate a metaphor that conceptualizes the ideal school.

Characteristics of a quality metaphor include images, sensory experiences, personal experiences, evoked emotions, creativity, and underlying values.

1. Using the value list generated at the last meeting, review each of the values listed. (5 minutes)

2. Discuss the metaphor and share. (10 minutes)

3. Use the list to create and develop another metaphor. (15 minutes)

Did the team:

- Share individual commitments to the safe school team?

- Develop an integrity checklist for the team?

- Generate a metaphor to create a shared vision?

Reflective Journal

Use this space to reflect on the third meeting. You may share these reflections during the first part of the next meeting.

_____

_____

_____

_____

_____

_____

_____

_____

_____

_____

_____

_____

_____

_____

_____

_____

_____

_____

_____

_____

_____

_____

_____

_____

_____

_____

_____

_____

_____

_____

_____

Fourth Meeting: Belief Systems

Approximate Meeting Length: 🕐 **One Hour**

See *LSS*, pp. 63-69

Meeting Goals

Goal 1: Understand empowering and limiting beliefs.

Goal 2: Use the belief system to build confidence among school community members in developing an effective strategy.

Goal 3: Complete a three-part confidence check relating to school leadership.

A belief system refers to the part of the mind that interprets messages, either external or internal, and perceives them as real. A belief is the mental acceptance and conviction that something exists. An acceptance shapes ones actions. Therefore, beliefs define many of our outcomes. A belief is a powerful tool for change but can become limiting when it prevents someone from achieving his/her full potential.

Activity One (🕐 20 Minutes)

Share a success story. This activity builds group confidence.

Begin by sharing a personal success story; ask the team member to your right to share his/her success story.

Activity Two (5 Minutes)

Members reflect on the following questions:

1. **Do I have something important to contribute to the development of a safe school?**

2. **Do I feel this task is important?**

3. **Do I desire to be part of this process?**

4. **Have my background and training led me to believe that this is where I belong?**

Appoint someone to write responses on newsprint. Use one sheet of newsprint for each member.

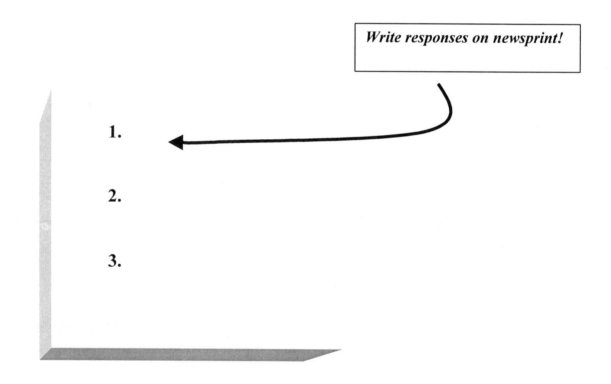

Write responses on newsprint!

1.

2.

3.

Activity Three ( 20 Minutes)

See *LSS*, pp. 70-76

Complete the three-part confidence check.

- **Allow free discussion of the checklist.**

- **Use the checklist for reflection.**

The Three-Part Confidence Check

| Confidence in the Leader | Confidence in the Vision | Self-Confidence |

Part 1: Confidence in the Leader

1. The leader works effectively with team members.
Yes　　　　*Maybe*　　　　*No*
2. Team members can recall successes under the leader's direction.
Yes　　　　*Maybe*　　　　*No*
3. Team members respect the leader.
Yes　　　　*Maybe*　　　　*No*
4. Team members seek to participate with the leader on challenging projects.
Yes　　　　*Maybe*　　　　*No*

Part 2: Confidence in the Vision

1. The leader has a clear vision of effective safe school practices. *Yes*   *Maybe*   *No*
2. The leader communicates a clear vision of a safe school environment. *Yes*   *Maybe*   *No*
3. Team members embrace the school leader's vision of a safe school environment. *Yes*   *Maybe*   *No*
4. Team members feel guided by the school leader's vision of a safe school environment. *Yes*   *Maybe*   *No*

Part 3: Self-Confidence

1. Does the team communicate confidence that they can provide a safe and secure environment? *Yes*   *Maybe*   *No*
2. Do the team's vocabulary, agenda, actions, and attitudes communicate confidence? *Yes*   *Maybe*   *No*
3. Is the school community aware of the team's successes? *Yes*   *Maybe*   *No*
4. Is the team working with confidence in their ability? *Yes*   *Maybe*   *No*

CONFIDENCE IS THE KEY TO SUCCESS *CONFIDENCE BREEDS CONFIDENCE*

LEADER: Follow-up:

See *LSS*, pp. 70-74

Ask each member to complete the following self-assessments before the next meeting. The team will reflect upon the assessments in the next meeting.

Domain 1: *Social Skills: Identify High Degree of Social Skills*

Current Strength	Yes	No
1. I have a high degree of comfort in interacting with people of diverse backgrounds.		
2. I communicate effectively with people of diverse backgrounds.		
3. I listen with understanding to people of diverse backgrounds.		
4. I meaningfully involve people from diverse backgrounds.		

> *Effective Teams Focus Solely on the Strengths Each Member Brings to the Team*

Domain 2: *Decision Making: Identify High Degree of Decision Making Skills*

Current Strength	Yes	No
1. I make excellent decisions under stress.		
2. I make collaborative decisions.		
3. I generate alternatives before making a decision.		
4. I collect information before making a decision.		

Domain 3: *Problem Solving: The Ability to Identify the Cause and the Source of Problems*

Current Strength	Yes	No
1. I accurately identify the correct problem.		
2. I locate and identify the source of a problem.		
3. I distinguish causes from symptoms associated with problems.		
4. I solve problems collaboratively, involving people affected by the problem and potential solutions.		

Don't be confused by symptoms. Look for the cause and select discover the real problem.

Domain 4: *Judgment: Identification of Ability to Make Sound Judgments*

Current Strength	Yes	No
1. I make sound judgments.		
2. I make accurate judgments of situations.		
3. I have the wisdom to know when to change direction.		
4. I have integrity-driven judgment.		

Domain 5: *Follow Through: Identification of the Ability to Follow Through*

Current Strength	Yes	No
1. I follow through on commitments.		
2. I manage time to complete responsibilities.		
3. I complete tasks with little or no supervision.		
4. I determine what is required and then act decisively.		

Did the team:

- Share a success story from their life?

- Understand empowering and limiting beliefs?

- Use the belief system to build confidence among school community members in developing an effective strategy?

- Complete a three part confidence check relating to school leadership?

- Understand the assignment for the next meeting?

Reflective Journal

Use this space to reflect on the fourth meeting. You may share these reflections during the first part of the next meeting.

_____
_____
_____
_____
_____
_____
_____
_____
_____
_____
_____
_____
_____
_____
_____
_____
_____
_____
_____
_____
_____
_____
_____
_____
_____
_____
_____
_____

Fifth Meeting: Shaping the Belief System Vision and Mission Statements

Approximate Meeting Length: 75 minutes

Meeting Goals

Goal 1: Examine the self-assessments completed since the last meeting.

Goal 2: Evaluate community suggestions.

Goal 3: Create an effective vision of a safe school.

Goal 4: Develop a mission statement.

Activity One (15 Minutes)

Evaluate self-assessments and identify the team's strengths and challenges in each of the five domains (see LSS, pp. 71-72).

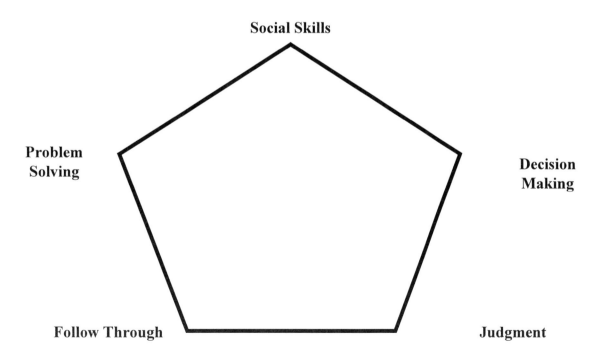

Now that you've completed assessing the five domains ...

1. Tally the team's strengths in each of the five domains.

2. Highlight the team's strengths.

3. Tally the team's challenges in each of the five domains.

4. Highlight the team's challenges.

5. Identify school and/or community members that can help address the team's challenges and strengthen the team.

6. Recruit these members to the team.

Activity Two (20 Minutes)

Brainstorm suggestions for a safe school environment.

1.

2.

3.

4.

5.

6.

Rate each suggestion according to its viability and perceived effectiveness.

1.

2.

3.

4.

5.

6.

7.

Assess Suggestions and Effectiveness Ratings for a Safe School Environment

Suggestion	Effective	Moderately Effective	Somewhat Effective	Not Too Effective	Scrap the Suggestion

Activity Three: Creating a Vision (20 Minutes).

See *LSS*, pp. 84-86

Develop a clear vision statement for your safe school plan.

A vision is a definite picture of a desired future. Developing a shared vision should entail four components: 1) knowing your context, 2) involving essential players, 3) seeing the future, and 4) committing it to writing. The vision needs to be achievable and aligned with the school community's shared values.

According to the North Central Regional Educational Laboratory, a vision illustrates what the school will be like in the future, incorporates deeply held values, is attainable, provides community members with hope, and becomes more real the more it is communicated.[1]

Make Sure:

Your vision inspires.

Your vision challenges.

Your vision empowers.

Your vision is believable.

NOW, DREAM, DREAM, DREAM OF THE IDEAL SAFE SCHOOL.

---

[1] Components of a Vision," North Central Regional Educational Laboratory, <http://www.ncrel.org/sdrs/areas/issues/educatrs/leadrshp/le1comps.htm > (23 May 2001).

Brainstorm the school's future design.

1. Talk about each description.
2. Identify the values, aspirations, and challenges inherent in each description.
3. Make sure each description is clear and concise.
4. List each clear description on a chart tablet.
5. Achieve consensus on a vision.

Record your team's vision statement here.

_____
_____
_____
_____
_____
_____
_____

Activity Four: Creating a Mission Statement (20 Minutes)

See *LSS*, pp. 87-88

An effective mission statement creates a sense of focus and gives the community the ability to discard distractions and set clear, identifiable, attainable priorities.

The Mission is The Map

See *LSS*, pp. 89-90

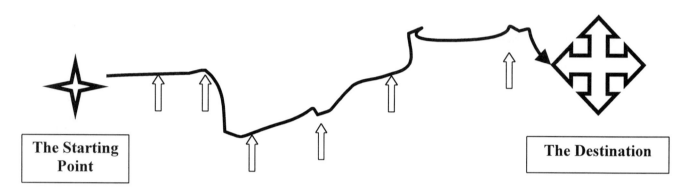

The Starting Point

The Destination

Each arrow represents a separate mission as the organization moves toward fulfillment of its mission.

Record each mission necessary to fulfill the vision.

Mission 1	
Mission 2	
Mission 3	
Mission 4	
Mission 5	
Mission 6	

Goals Leading to Mission Attainment

- Identify five concise, attainable goals to achieve each mission.
- Include a time-line and assign a member to be accountable for each goal.

Mission 1: _____

Goal	Time-line for Achievement	Person Responsible

Mission 2: _____

Goal	Time-line for Achievement	Person Responsible

Mission 3: _____

Goal	Time-line for Achievement	Person Responsible

Mission 4: _____

Goal	Time-line for Achievement	Person Responsible

Mission 5: _____

Goal	Time-line for Achievement	Person Responsible

Mission 6: _____

Goal	Time-line for Achievement	Person Responsible

Record goal and mission accomplishment on the integrity board. Frequently update the integrity board.

Integrity Board

We Made a Commitment and Saw It Through

Person Responsible for Goal	Completion Statement
Maria Ortiz	*I contacted five community members and successfully recruited them as members of our task force.*
Bob Johnson	*I conducted four focus groups at local churches to get community input for the safe school plan.*
Mark Ripowski	*I coordinated the flow of information from the team to the school faculty through a weekly newsletter.*
Kathy Obello	*I met with student leaders weekly, seeking their input for the safe school plan.*
Rev. Jack Smith	*I organized the pastors from the various churches in the community as a means of building grassroots support for the safe school plan.*

Did the team:

- Examine the self-assessments completed since the last meeting?
- Evaluate community suggestions?
- Create an effective vision of a safe school?
- Develop a mission statement?

Reflective Journal

Use this space to reflect on the fifth meeting. You may share these reflections during the first part of the next meeting.

_____
_____
_____
_____
_____
_____
_____
_____
_____
_____
_____
_____
_____
_____
_____
_____
_____
_____
_____
_____
_____
_____
_____
_____
_____
_____
_____
_____
_____

Sixth Meeting: Benchmarking and SWOT Analysis

Approximate Meeting Length: One Hour

Meeting Goals

Goal 1: Complete a SWOT analysis for your school.

Goal 2: Identify and apply appropriate benchmarks.

Activity One (30 Minutes)

LEADER: In this activity, work with the team to complete a SWOT analysis (see *LSS*, pp. 90-92).

S- Strengths: *Refers to the current effective strategies that address instructional, safety, and social issues.*

W- Weaknesses: *Refers to the ineffectiveness of current strategies and tactics in addressing safe schools.*

O- Opportunities: *Refers to the potential opportunities coming from the successful implementation of the safe school. These serve as motivational benchmarks for the school.*

T- Threats: *Refers to potential events such as terrorist attacks, kidnapping, hostage situations, or incidences of extreme violence.*

Apply The SWOT To Your School

Divide the team into four groups.

Assign an area (S, W, O, and T) to each group and identify specific examples of each particular area. Reconvene and record each group's findings on the following chart.

Strengths	Weaknesses
Opportunities	**Threats**

Each group member is responsible for sharing the group's findings with other members of the school community and seeking feedback of potential gaps in the analysis. Members report identified gaps at the next meeting.

Activity Two (30 Minutes)

In this activity, you will create benchmarks for your school programs (see LSS, pp. 95-103).

- **Divide the team into four groups.**

- **Each group explores the four benchmark types and applies them to the school.**

- **Reconvene the team to report findings.**

Organizational Benchmarking

List the following benchmarks.

Potential best practices from other district schools:

_____
_____
_____
_____

Schools that increased student performance:

_____
_____
_____
_____

Competitive Benchmarking

List several high-achieving schools and identify characteristics of each school that make it high-achieving.

School	Characteristics

Unilateral Benchmarking

List several facilities or organizations (outside education) that utilize best practices.

Organization or Program	Practices

Futuristic Benchmarking

In this activity, the team will analyze how the twelve trends of the future of education will affect the school.[1]

Trend 1: There will be a renewed focus on curriculum and instruction.

This will affect our campus by:

_____

_____

Trend 2: There will be an increased emphasis on standards and accountability.

This will affect our campus by:

_____

_____

Trend 3: There will be increased enrollment of minority, poor, and special education students.

This will affect our campus by:

_____

_____

Trend 4: There will be instability and unpredictable resource allocations.
This will affect our campus by:

_____

_____

Trend 5: There will be changing roles in school and community decision-making processes.

This will affect our campus by:

_____

_____

---

[1] "Trends Impacting Northwest Education," *Annual Report,* Northwest Regional Education Laboratory (1998), <http://www.nwrel.org/comm/1997ar/3.html > (27 March 2000).

Trend 6: There will be increased disparity between rich and poor communities.

This will affect our campus by:

_____

_____

Trend 7: There will be increased state involvement in local education decisions.

This will affect our campus by:

_____

_____

Trend 8: There will be increased competition for existing public funds.

This will affect our campus by:

_____

_____

Trend 9: There will be increased demand by the public for greater participation in the educational process.

This will affect our campus by:

_____

_____

Trend 10: There will be increased integration of available services to meet the needs of the children.

This will affect our campus by:

_____

_____

Trend 11: The gap between rich and poor families will increase.
This will affect our campus by:

_____

_____

Trend 12: Barriers related to full achievement for all students will remain.

This will affect our campus by:

_____

_____

Did the Team:

- **Complete a SWOT analysis for your school?**
- **Identify and apply appropriate benchmarks?**

Reflective Journal

Use this space to reflect on the sixth meeting. You may share these reflections during the first part of the next meeting.

_____

_____

_____

_____

_____

_____

_____

_____

_____

_____

_____

_____

_____

_____

_____

_____

_____

_____

_____

_____

_____

_____

_____

_____

_____

_____

_____

_____

_____

_____

Seventh Meeting: Consensus Building

Approximate Meeting Length: 30 Minutes

Meeting Goals

Goal 1: Fill in the gaps in the SWOT analysis.

Goal 2: Identify the precise conditions of the current environment.

Goal 3: Develop plans for collection of pertinent data related to the current environment.

Activity One (20 minutes)

- *Revisit the SWOT analysis and fill in the gaps.*

- *Members share their findings and report them as a team.*

Activity Two (10 minutes)

- *Review the data collection process and assign responsibility to members to gather data.*

- *Record and review the responsibilities for gathering data.*

Data Gap (Data Still Needed)	Person Responsible for Collecting Data
Student cohort completion rate	*Marcia Jones, assistant principal*

Integrity Board

Person Responsible for Goal	Completion Statement
Maria Ortiz	*I contacted five community members and successfully recruited them as members of our task force.*
Bob Johnson	*I conducted four focus groups at local churches to get community input for the safe school plan.*
Mark Ripowski	*I coordinated the flow of information from the team to the school faculty through a weekly newsletter.*
Kathy Obello	*I met with student leaders weekly, seeking their input for the safe school plan.*
Rev. Jack Smith	*I organized the pastors from the various churches in the community as a means of building grassroots support for the safe school plan.*
Marcia Jones, assistant principal.	*I collected data related to the student cohort completion rate and presented it to the group.*

Person Responsible for Goal	Completion Statement

Review the following responsibilities for gathering data.

1. **Interview community, staff, and students.**

2. **Review numbers and historical data from school records.**

3. **Create a needs assessment survey.**

    -   **Each needs assessment survey should have at least three items worded in a negative pattern, in addition to positive statements.**
    -   **Score each statement on a five-point Likert scale (i.e., strongly agree, agree, no opinion, disagree, strongly disagree).**
    -   **Target the appropriate population to increase the likelihood of receiving accurate and appropriate data.**

- **Develop a needs assessment with sensitivity toward various cultures in the community (i.e., translate into dominate languages represented in the community).**

Identify the persons responsible for the following data (teams of two or more).

Persons Responsible	Data Collected
1. 2.	*Employee background checks*
1. 2.	*Patterns of teacher discipline referrals*
1. 2.	*The community culture*
1. 2.	*Administrative and teacher response to problems and potential problems*
1. 2.	*Identification of symptoms of disorder, potential violence, and related issues*
1. 2.	*Crisis preparation*

Did the team:

- **Fill in the gaps in the SWOT analysis?**

- **Identify the precise conditions of the current environment?**

- **Develop plans for collection of pertinent data related to the current environment?**

Reflective Journal

Use this space to reflect on the seventh meeting. You may share these reflections during the first part of the next meeting. Possible journal topic: Reflect on the data gathered.

_____
_____
_____
_____
_____
_____
_____
_____
_____
_____
_____
_____
_____
_____
_____
_____
_____
_____
_____
_____
_____
_____
_____
_____
_____
_____
_____
_____

Eighth Meeting: Gaining Agreement

Approximate Meeting Length: 65 Minutes

See *LSS*, pp. 107-110

Meeting Goals

Goal 1: Revisit the data collection process.

Goal 2: Identify areas of concern and strength.

Goal 3: Identify points of reconciliation and contention.

Activity One (30 Minutes)

Revisit the data collection process. Each group reports their findings.

Remember to:

1. Trust the experience of the other team members.
2. Listen to the members of the school and community.
3. Lower personal defenses and reactions.
4. Ask questions to gain clarification.
5. Take personal responsibility for making the relationship work.
6. Act to heal conflict.

Group	Data

Activity Two (15 Minutes)

Facilitate discussion based on areas of:

- **strengths**
- **concern**
- **Other's experiences**

Identify the areas of strengths in the school based on data gathering (include any experiences members of the community have shared).

1.	
2.	
3.	
4.	
5.	

Identify the areas of concern in the school based on data gathering (include any experiences members of the community have shared).

1.	
2.	
3.	
4.	
5.	

Identify the experiences shared by members of the team.

1.
2.
3.
4.
5.

Activity Three (20 Minutes)

In this activity have the team:

1. **Clarify perceptions.**
2. **Identify personal views of safe schools.**
3. **Identify points of reconciliation.**
4. **Identify points of contention.**

Did the team:

- **Revisit the data collection process?**

- **Identify areas of concern and strength?**

- **Identify points of reconciliation and contention?**

Reflective Journal

Use this space to reflect on the eighth meeting. You may share these reflections during the first part of the next meeting. Possible topic: How would you rate the importance (urgency) of the areas identified by the team?

_____
_____
_____
_____
_____
_____
_____
_____
_____
_____
_____
_____
_____
_____
_____
_____
_____
_____
_____
_____
_____
_____
_____
_____
_____
_____
_____
_____
_____

Ninth Meeting: Building the Knowledge Base

Approximate Meeting Length: One Hour

See *LSS*, Chapter 7, pp. 131-158

Meeting Goals

Goal 1: Review the characteristics of a safe school.

Goal 2: Apply Maslow's needs hierarchy to the school context in determining priorities.

Goal 3: Develop a parental involvement model.

Activity One (40 Minutes)

In this activity, review the characteristics of a safe school and determine whether the characteristics exist at this campus.

- **Divide the team into two groups.**

- **Each group will complete the assigned assessment.**

Group One: Based on *Early Warning, Timely Response: A Guide to Safe Schools*[1]

Safe School Characteristic	Rating Scale: 1 = Nonexistent; 10 = Clearly Present
Focus on academic achievement	1 2 3 4 5 6 7 8 9 10
Include the families of students in important ways	1 2 3 4 5 6 7 8 9 10
Develop important connections among students and adults in the school community	1 2 3 4 5 6 7 8 9 10
Openly discuss issues of safety with students, teachers, parents, and community members	1 2 3 4 5 6 7 8 9 10
Provide environments where all students are treated equally	1 2 3 4 5 6 7 8 9 10
Encourage and allow students to share their feelings to school personnel	1 2 3 4 5 6 7 8 9 10
Have a system in place that quickly refers children when there is suspicion of abuse or neglect	1 2 3 4 5 6 7 8 9 10
Offer extended-day programs	1 2 3 4 5 6 7 8 9 10
Promote exemplary citizenship and character	1 2 3 4 5 6 7 8 9 10
Recognize problems and evaluate progress toward solutions	1 2 3 4 5 6 7 8 9 10
Advocate for students transitioning from student to adult life and entering the workforce	1 2 3 4 5 6 7 8 9 10
Stress positive connections among students and adults in the school environment	1 2 3 4 5 6 7 8 9 10
Provide avenues for students to share their concerns with adults in the school	1 2 3 4 5 6 7 8 9 10

---

[1] Early Warning, Timely Response: A Guide to Safe Schools, referenced ed., Center for Effective Collaboration and Practices (1999), <http://www.air-dc.org/cecp/guide/annotated.htm> (5 April 2000).

Group Two: Based on Kathleen Cotton's "Schoolwide and Classroom Discipline"[1]

Safe School Characteristic	Description	√
Commitment to establish and maintain high standards of behavior for learning	<ul><li>All members of the community work to achieve the same end</li><li>High level of commitment to achieve goals</li><li>Shared belief that high levels of student instructional performance relate directly to maintaining high standards</li></ul>	
High behavioral expectations	<ul><li>Expectations are clear</li><li>School leader communicates expectations</li><li>Administrators and teachers share a common set of high expectations for student behavior and performance</li></ul>	
Clear and broad-based rules	<ul><li>Rules, penalties, and processes have broad-based input</li><li>Rules, penalties, and processes are communicated</li><li>Administrators and teachers follow rules, penalties, and processes</li><li>There is no ambiguity</li></ul>	
Warm school climate	<ul><li>There is a deep concern by administrators and teachers for students as individuals</li><li>Student issues are paramount</li><li>Administrators identify the needs of students</li><li>Teachers relate directly to the students</li><li>People care for each other</li></ul>	
Visible, supportive principal	<ul><li>Principal is visible in hallways and classrooms</li><li>Principal knows students by names</li><li>Principal expresses interest in students' lives</li><li>Principal is supportive of teachers' needs</li></ul>	
Close ties with the community	<ul><li>Partnerships established with the school community</li><li>Parents are involved with school activities</li><li>Parents and the school community are informed of school issues, goals, and activities</li><li>The school acts inclusively toward members of the community</li></ul>	
Delegation of discipline authority to teachers	<ul><li>Principals handle serious discipline cases</li><li>Teachers have authority and responsibility to handle routine classroom discipline problems</li><li>Principals work with teachers to improve management skills</li></ul>	

[1] Kathleen Cotton, "Schoolwide and Classroom Discipline," *School Improvement Research Series* (SIRS), Close-Up #9 (December 1990), Northwest Regional Educational Laboratory <http://www.nwrel.org/scpd/sirs/5/cu9/html> (3 March 1999)

What Did We Learn?

1.

2.

3.

4.

5.

Activity Two (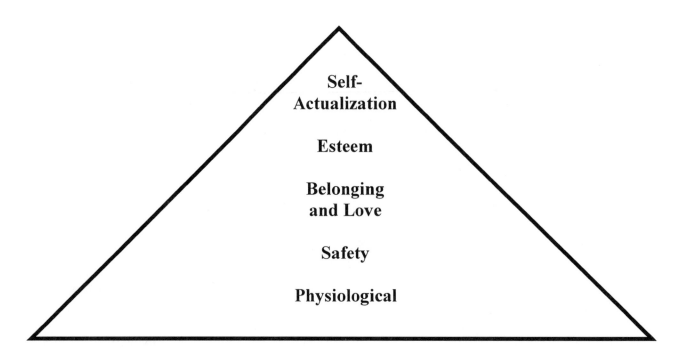 20 Minutes)

In this activity, identify the areas of concern and how they fit into Maslow's hierarchy of needs. See *LSS*, pp. 147-151.

Self-
Actualization

Esteem

Belonging
and Love

Safety

Physiological

Use the hierarchy of needs pyramid to determine which needs must be addressed.

Immediate Needs to Address

1.

2.

3.

4.

5.

6.

7.

Did the team:

- **Review the characteristics of a safe school?**
- **Apply Maslow's needs hierarchy to the school context in determining priorities?**
- **Develop a parental involvement model?**

Reflective Journal

Use this space to reflect on the ninth meeting. You may share these reflections during the first part of the next meeting. Possible journal topic: Are safe schools related to the curriculum taught in the school?

_____
_____
_____
_____
_____
_____
_____
_____
_____
_____
_____
_____
_____
_____
_____
_____
_____
_____
_____
_____
_____
_____
_____
_____
_____

Tenth Meeting: Reducing the Risk, Part I

Approximate Meeting Length: 40 Minutes

See *LSS*, pp. 159-160

Meeting Goals

Goal 1: Identify common labels used to isolate certain individuals or groups from the campus community as a whole.

Goal 2: Determine which labels are essential, which have a negative meaning, and which have a positive meaning within the school's culture.

Goal 3: Map some examples as to how such labels produce specific behaviors in students, parents, and teachers.

Goal 4: Determine specific strategies to change the systemic behavior created by negative labels.

Activity One 40 Minutes

See *LSS*, pp. 160-163

Labels are powerful. Labels can fragment a campus or build a community of learners. This exercise will help the team determine what labels are currently used to describe people or groups within the school.

Record the brainstorming outcomes of the identification of the different types of students or student groups on campus.

1.

2.

3.

4.

5.

6.

7.

Identify the types of parents.

1.

2.

3.

4.

5.

6.

7.

Identify the types of faculty and staff members.

1.

2.

3.

4.

5.

6.

7.

Gain consensus on important and necessary labels and harmful labels.

All labels have some usefulness in communication as shorthand for a set of assumed attributes; one danger, however, is stereotyping an individual with attributes he does not possess. After reaching agreement on essential labels, apply that definition and mark each label listed with E for essential or N for not essential.

- Poll all members at the meeting as to whether the label is positive (thumbs up) or negative (thumbs down).

- Record the number of people indicating positive and the number indicating negative next to each essential label.

- After recording the vote for each essential label, determine which labels did not have a consensus either positive or negative.

- Ask one person to briefly explain each point of view.

Did the team:

- Identify common labels used to isolate certain individuals or groups from the campus community as whole?

- Determine which labels are essential, which have a negative meaning, and which have a positive meaning within the school's culture?

- Map some examples as to how such labels affect students, parents, and teachers?

- Determine specific strategies to change the systemic behavior created by negative labels?

Reflective Journal

Use this space to reflect on the tenth meeting. You may share these reflections during the first part of the next meeting. Possible journal topic: What labels do I use everyday that may affect the lives of those around me?

_____

_____

_____

_____

_____

_____

_____

_____

_____

_____

_____

_____

_____

_____

_____

_____

_____

_____

_____

_____

_____

_____

_____

_____

Eleventh Meeting: Reducing the Risk, Part II

Approximate Meeting Length: One Hour

See *LSS*, pp. 163-167

Meeting Goals

Goal 1: Reach a consensus on the type of community you want to align for your school.

Goal 2: Understand the necessary elements to build a spirit of community.

Activity One (40 minutes)

LEADER: Achieve consensus as to the definition of a community.

1. On an index card, each team member will write a brief (one or two sentence) definition of community.

2. When everyone finishes writing his/her definition, pair team members. Each team member shares his/her definition with his/her team partner.

3. Each pair develops a collaborative definition.

4. Each pair joins another pair and repeats the process until the entire group creates a comprehensive definition of community.

Activity Two ( 20 Minutes)

Community spirit arises from community members working toward a common goal, acting with integrity, moving toward dialogue, and inviting and respecting the ideas and viewpoints of all other community members.

Provide examples of how members exhibit integrity (list what and when).

1.

2.

3.

4.

5.

6.

Provide specific examples of how different members moved toward dialogue in accomplishing the goals of the group.

1.

2.

3.

4.

5.

6.

7.

8.

9.

10.

Provide specific examples of how all views were included in the discussion.

1.

2.

3.

4.

5.

6.

7.

8.

9.

10.

Provide specific examples of respect given to multiple viewpoints.

1.

2.

3.

4.

5.

6.

7.

8.

9.

10.

Translate what you have learned to the daily activities of the school community.

1.

2.

3.

4.

5.

6.

7.

8.

9.

10.

Did the team:

- **Reach a consensus on the type of community you want to build for your school?**

- **Understand the necessary elements to build a spirit of community?**

Reflective Journal

Use this space to reflect on the eleventh meeting. You may share these reflections during the first part of the next meeting. Possible journal topic: What can I do to foster a sense of community in the school?

_____
_____
_____
_____
_____
_____
_____
_____
_____
_____
_____
_____
_____
_____
_____
_____
_____
_____
_____
_____
_____
_____
_____
_____
_____

Twelfth Meeting: At-Risk Behaviors

Approximate Meeting Length: 70 Minutes

See *LSS*, pp. 167-180

Meeting Goals

Goal 1: Identify at-risk behaviors and assess the level of risk.

Goal 2: Identify threshold standards for behavior.

Goal 3: Coordinate the collection of additional safe school/safe classroom resources.

Activity One (30 Minutes)

Identifying at-risk behaviors is a complex task since individuals often respond differently to the same set of conditions. These differences come from previous experience, family socialization, or cultural diversity. A student's response to circumstances causes at-risk behavior. Furthermore, these response patterns become structured ways of acting. The more frequently the child responds using these patterns, the more automatic these responses become. Finally, as these behavior patterns become automatic, they become unconscious.

LEADER: Divide the team into groups of three or four people. The task for each group is to brainstorm response patterns that lead to at-risk behavior as possible within a twenty-minute period.

Example of a Response Pattern Creating At-Risk Conditions

Student Action	Response Pattern
Child is stressed, comes to class late.	Teacher confronts student about tardiness.
Child responds with a curt reply.	The teacher reacts by reprimanding the child for disrespect/indifference.
Child becomes frustrated with the teacher's response and raises his or her voice in the power struggle.	Teacher becomes angry and punishes the child.
Child verbally or physically abuses the teacher.	Child is removed from campus and declared emotionally disturbed.

Ask each group to share the at-risk response patterns identified with the others and as a large group.

- Assign a number between one and ten to the pattern to indicate the probability of its development.

- A response of one indicates that the response is likely to occur only one out of ten instances. A response of ten indicates that the response is likely to occur ten out of ten times.

Activity Two (30 Minutes)

Threshold standards of behavior represent the degree to which the school community chooses to tolerate specific behaviors. An awareness of threshold standards of behavior is essential for comprehending and reducing the patterns of events that lead to violent and abusive behavior.

LEADER: Brainstorm and discuss the various standards of behavior for students, parents and teachers.

Identify the actual (not the desired) standard.

1.

2.

3.

4.

5.

6.

7.

8.

9.

Is the standard clearly articulated?

1.

2.

3.

4.

5.

6.

7.

8.

9.

10.

Is the standard universally applied?

1.

2.

3.

4.

5.

6.

7.

8.

9.

10.

What are the rationales for applying it differently?

1.

2.

3.

4.

5.

6.

7.

8.

9.

10.

For the list of standards:

**Are there any standards that create barriers
toward achieving our community goals?**

1.

2.

3.

4.

5.

6.

7.

8.

9.

10.

Should any standards be replaced with standards that more efficiently facilitate goal achievement? Should any standards be added to the list?

1.

2.

3.

4.

5.

6.

7.

8.

9.

10.

Activity 3 (10 Minutes)

See *LSS*, pp. 173-181

LEADER: Collect information and report to the whole group (use the following subtopics as a guide).

- Early warning signs of school violence
- Intervention techniques for specific individuals/situations
- Meaningful parental involvement
- Meaningful student involvement
- Characteristics of a safe physical environment
- Characteristics of effective policies and practices that support individual responsibility
- Characteristics of responsive schools
- Crisis planning and practice
- Resources for the classroom teacher

Web Sites

The following is a listing of Web sites containing information about building classroom and school communities or safe schools. This list is not complete; it is a starting place for the team.

www.waveamerica.com
www.ncsu.edu/cpsv
www.safeschools.org
www.nsscl.org
members.tripod.com/~twood/guide.html
www.pledge.org
eric-web.tc.columbia.edu/monographs/uds107/preventing-contents.hml
eric-web.tc.columbia.edu/monographs/uds107/gang-contents.hml
www.mentalhealth.org/schoolviolence/
www.mcpc.org/2sch/103.htm
www.ed.gov/offices/OSER/OSEP/earlywrn.html
www.keepschoolssafe.org

www.ucsc.edu/currents/99-00/03-05/opinion.html
eric-web.tc.columbia.edu/monographs/uds107/school-contents.htm
www.theiacp.org/pubinfo/pubs/pslc/suindex.htm
www.ed.gov/pubs/annschoolrept98/
www.rippleeffects.com/needs/
www2.ncsu.edu/ncsu/cep/previolence/eoto98.htm
www.mentalhealth.org./newsroom/schoolviolencearchieves.htm
helping.apa.org/warningsigns/index.html
www.splcenter.org/teachingtolerance/tt-index.html
www.usdoj.gov/kidspage/bias-k-5/teacher.htm

Did the team:

- **Identify at-risk behaviors and assess the level of risk?**

- **Identify threshold standards for behavior?**

- **Coordinate the collection of additional safe school/safe classroom resources?**

Reflective Journal

Use this space to reflect on the twelfth meeting. You may share these reflections during the first part of the next meeting. Possible journal topic: Are there instances of at risk behavior I tend to ignore?

_____
_____
_____
_____
_____
_____
_____
_____
_____
_____
_____
_____
_____
_____
_____
_____
_____
_____
_____
_____
_____
_____
_____
_____
_____
_____
_____

Thirteenth Meeting: Drafting the Plan

Approximate Meeting Length: One Hour

See *LSS*, pp. 183-192

Meeting Goals

Goal 1: Discuss and share the specific information collected about safe schools.

Goal 2: Identify the major sections of the plan.

Goal 3: Elect an editor of the plan, define his/her role, and assign responsibility for drafting a specific section of the plan to specific individuals.

Activity One (30 Minutes)

LEADER: Ask each member to present a brief synopsis of the major points found in his or her research of the assigned subtopic.

Major Points

1.

2.

3.

4.

5.

6.

7.

Activity Two (20 Minutes)

LEADER: Brainstorm the possible sections or topics to including the plan.

1.

2.

3.

4.

5.

6.

7.

8.

9.

10.

Before voting on the inclusion of each section or topic, have the group determine the criteria for acceptance—simple majority vote, two-thirds vote, or consensus. After appropriate discussion, the group accepts or rejects each section or topic.

Activity Three (10 Minutes)

LEADER: Ask each member to discuss the responsibilities of the editor of the plan.

Record these responses on the integrity board and take a quick vote for each item. A simple majority will determine the responsibilities of the editor.

Once the responsibilities of the editor are established, members of the team will nominate individuals to serve as editor. The individual, however, will have the right to decline a nomination once the process is complete. Each member will vote by secret ballot. Simple majority will determine the winner.

Assign each individual on the team, with the exception of the editor, a section of the plan to write.

Member	Writing Assignment

Did the team:

- **Discuss and share the specific information collected about the safe schools?**

- **Identify the major sections of the plan?**

- **Elect an editor of the plan, define his/her role, and assign responsibility for drafting specific sections of the plan to specific individuals?**

Reflective Journal

Use this space to reflect on the thirteenth meeting. You may share these reflections during the first part of the next meeting. Possible journal topic: Reflect on the entire process of developing a safe school plan.

_____
_____
_____
_____
_____
_____
_____
_____
_____
_____
_____
_____
_____
_____
_____
_____
_____
_____
_____
_____
_____
_____
_____
_____
_____
_____
_____
_____

Fourteenth Meeting: Coalition Building

Approximate Meeting Length: 80 Minutes

See *LSS*, pp. 199-203

Meeting Goals

Goal 1: Identify multiple sources of support.

Goal 2: Build a successful coalition.

Goal 3: Plan the strategies for inviting full participation for community constituents and gaining approval of the plan.

Activity One (40 Minutes)

LEADER: Brainstorm the identity of the internal and external stakeholders within the extended school community (students, teachers, parents, staff members, business leaders, community agencies, central office staff, and local officials).

Write the title of the stakeholder on the list at the top of a sheet of newsprint, one per page. For example, write "Students" at the top of one sheet.

Students
1.
2.
3.
4.

Brainstorm and record all the components within that group. For example, sixth-grade students, boys, girls, football players, reading club members, and so forth. Do the same for each group.

Sixth-Grade Students
1.
2.
3.
4.
5.
6.
7.

Activity Two (10 Minutes)

LEADER: Ask team members to pair up to present the safe school plan to various members of each of the groups assigned to them from the listing.

The team members present a draft of the plan seeking to gain additional input.

Activity Three (30 Minutes)

LEADER: Brainstorm strategies to encourage community participation.

Rank the strategies.

Use these strategies to achieve broad-based support for the plan's implementation.

Ranking of Strategies

1.

2.

3.

4.

5.

6.

7.

8.

9.

Did the team:

- **Identify multiple sources of support?**

- **Build a successful coalition?**

- **Plan the strategies for inviting full participation for community constituents and gaining approval for the plan?**

Reflective Journal

Use this space to reflect on the final meeting.

_____
_____
_____
_____
_____
_____
_____
_____
_____
_____
_____
_____
_____
_____
_____
_____
_____
_____
_____
_____
_____
_____
_____
_____
_____
_____
_____
_____
_____

About the Author

Raymond L. Calabrese is a professor of Educational Leadership at Wichita State University, Kansas. Dr. Calabrese has significant public school administrative experience including work as an assistant principal, middle school principal, and high school principal. He is the author of five books focusing on school leadership and numerous articles for national and international journals. Dr. Calabrese can be reached by email at rlcalabrese@earthlink.net.